Emergency Aid

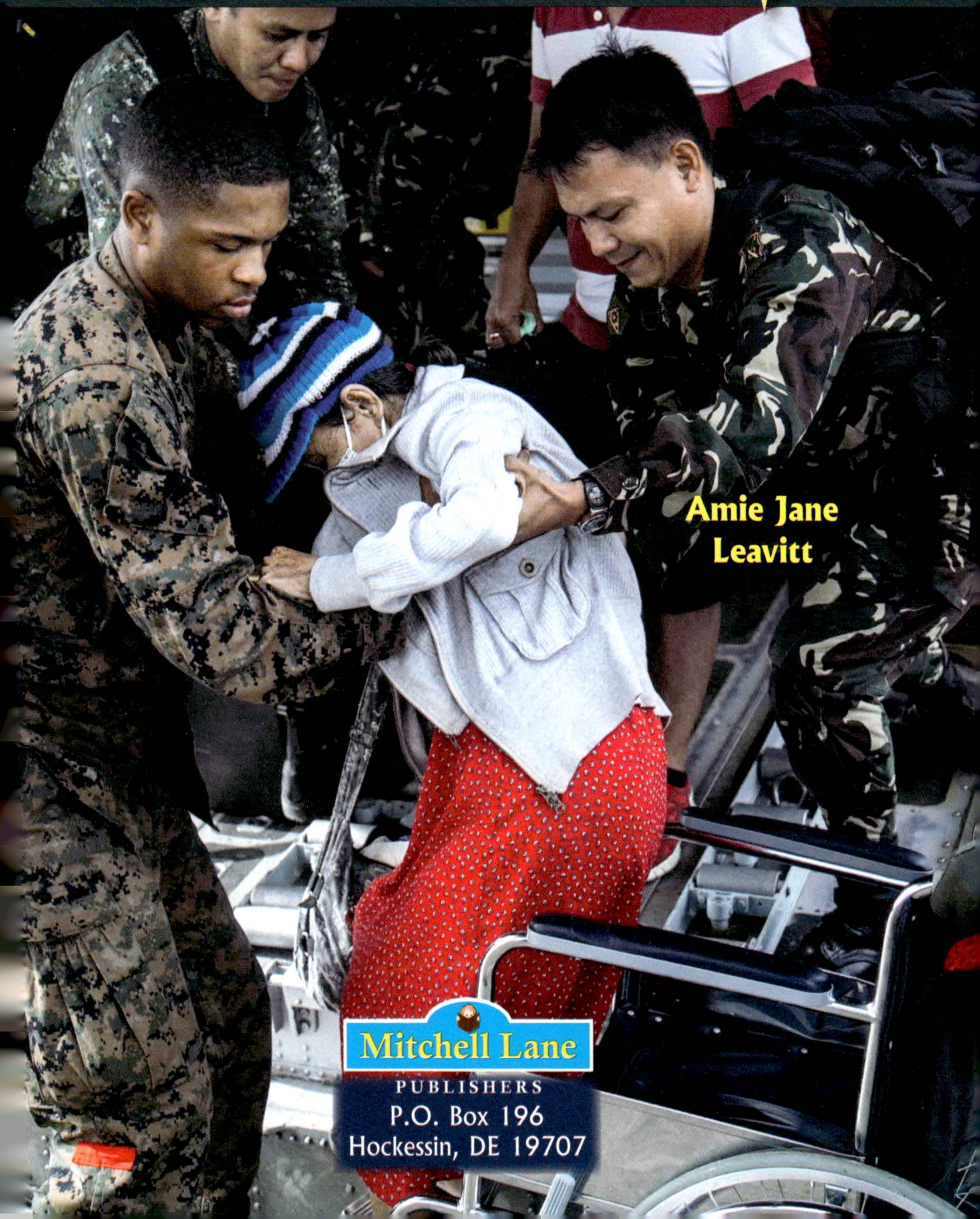

Amie Jane Leavitt

Mitchell Lane
PUBLISHERS
P.O. Box 196
Hockessin, DE 19707

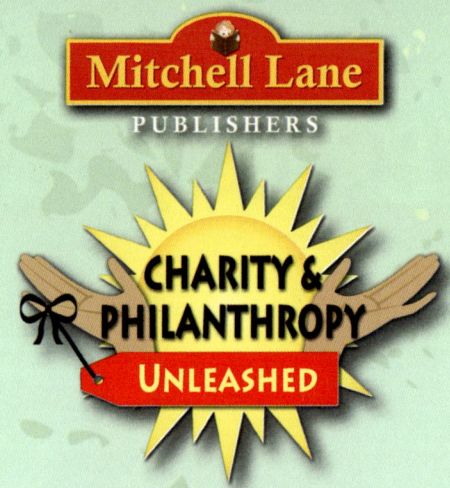

Conquering Disease
Emergency Aid
Environmental Protection
Helping Children with Life-Threatening Medical Issues
Helping Our Veterans
Preserving Human Rights Around the World
The Quest to End World Hunger
Support for Education

Copyright © 2015 by Mitchell Lane Publishers

All rights reserved. No part of this book may be reproduced without written permission from the publisher. Printed and bound in the United States of America.

PUBLISHER'S NOTE: The facts in this book have been thoroughly researched. Documentation of such research can be found on pages 44–45. While every possible effort has been made to ensure accuracy, the publisher will not assume liability for damages caused by inaccuracies in the data, and makes no warranty on the accuracy of the information contained herein.

The Internet sites referenced herein were active as of the publication date. Due to the fleeting nature of some web sites, we cannot guarantee that they will all be active when you are reading this book.

Printing 1 2 3 4 5 6 7 8 9

Library of Congress Cataloging-in-Publication Data

Leavitt, Amie Jane.
 Emergency aid / by Amie Jane Leavitt.
   pages cm. — (Charity and philanthropy unleashed)
 Includes bibliographical references and index.
 ISBN 978-1-61228-575-7 (library bound)
 1. Disaster relief—Juvenile literature.
 2. Charities—Juvenile literature. I. Title.
 HV553.L43 2015
 363.34'8—dc23
                                    2014008296

eBook ISBN: 9781612286136

PBP

Contents

Introduction	5
CHAPTER 1	
A LITTLE HELP WHEN IT'S NEEDED MOST	6
Millions of People Helped Every Year	13
CHAPTER 2	
WHERE THERE'S A NEED THERE'S A WAY	14
Reuniting with Loved Ones	21
CHAPTER 3	
TOP HELPERS	22
Symbols That Equal Help	29
CHAPTER 4	
GETTING PREPARED	30
Ham Radio to the Rescue	35
CHAPTER 5	
LENDING A HAND	36
Send in the Troops—The US Military Helps Out with Disaster Relief	41
What You Can Do To Help	42
Timeline	43
Further Reading	44
Books	44
On the Internet	44
Works Consulted	44
Glossary	46
Index	47

Introduction

According to the American Red Cross, more than 4.4 billion people have been affected by disasters in the last twenty years. Just think about that statistic for a minute: that's roughly three times the number of people living in China, the world's most populous country! Every year, approximately 200 million people (about the population of Brazil) are impacted in some way by disasters such as floods, hurricanes, volcanic eruptions, chemical spills, fires, tornadoes, tsunamis, typhoons, earthquakes, and droughts.

When disaster strikes, human beings seem to have an innate desire to help their neighbors in need. It doesn't matter if those "neighbors" literally live right next door, in another city or state, or on the other side of the globe. When a natural disaster happens, people immediately come together and start pooling their resources in order to help those who desperately need it.

CHAPTER 1
A Little Help When It's Needed Most

The date was February 29, 2012. In the middle of the night, a tornado snaked through the town of Branson, Missouri. It was an EF2 tornado, with winds between 120 and 130 miles per hour. When the tornado touched the ground, it stretched 400 yards across, which is the same size as four football fields extended end-to-end. EF2 tornadoes aren't the most severe tornadoes, but any tornado can cause a great amount of damage if it strikes the right area. And that was definitely the case with this Branson, Missouri, tornado.

Sections of the town were severely damaged. The tornado literally ripped things apart, picked them up, and flung them about. In places, the land looked more like a landfill than a town: debris, furniture, cars, and torn-apart houses were heaped together in giant mounds. Those who were unlucky enough to own a home in the path of the tornado lost everything. Their homes were destroyed. Their personal belongings were scattered about.

Immediately following the tornado, disaster relief organizations arrived on the scene. The specialists from these groups got in touch with the people who had lost their homes. They made sure they had a safe place to stay, food to eat, and personal hygiene items. The specialists also helped people reunite with their family members and contact their insurance companies to make the necessary claims.

CPR Training to the Rescue

Rewind back in time to November 2011. A seventeen-year-old named Reid Heiser was working at a community recreation

Branson, Missouri, is famous for its many theaters which are located on 76 Country Boulevard. The live shows in these theaters attract tourists, but many of these theaters (and their signs) were damaged in the 2012 tornado.

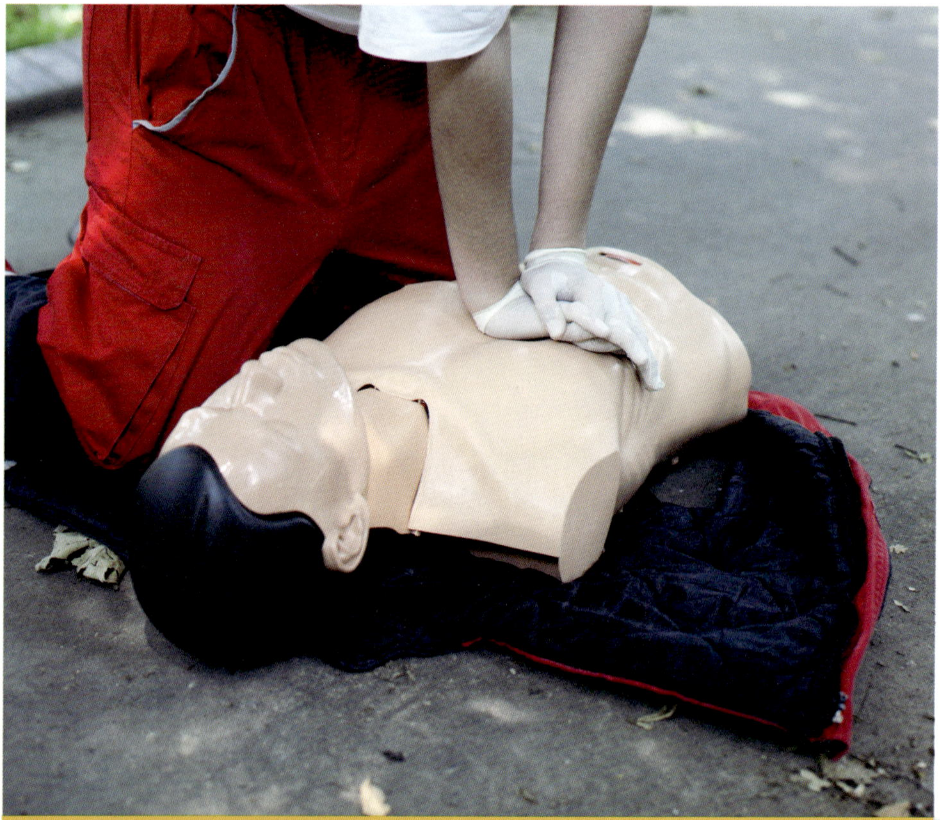

Chapter 1

 The Red Cross trains people all around the world in CPR so they will be prepared to help out in an emergency.

center in his hometown of Monroe, Michigan. Suddenly, a man named Jim Hammer collapsed as he was playing tennis. Reid rushed to Jim's side. Jim was unconscious and not breathing. Reid immediately started performing CPR (cardiopulmonary resuscitation) on Jim and kept at it until the paramedics arrived.

Fortunately, Reid had just taken a CPR class offered by the Red Cross the week before. He sure was grateful that he had taken this class so he could help Jim out in such a critical moment. Jim was most definitely glad, too. As he told the American Red Cross, "I wouldn't be here if it wasn't for this guy."

A LITTLE HELP WHEN IT'S NEEDED MOST

The Odisha super-cyclone of 1999 was the strongest recorded storm ever to hit the Indian subcontinent. This massive storm affected more than thirteen million people.

Many people like Reid are trained every day to conduct emergency medical procedures. And those procedures help save lives all over the world.

Advanced Preparation Saves Lives

On October 29, 1999, the Odisha super-cyclone spun across the Bay of Bengal and struck India with a vengeance. Wind speeds exceeded 160 miles per hour, making this storm the strongest to ever hit the subcontinent. Trees were wrenched out of the ground. Roofs were snapped off and catapulted miles away. Power lines were twisted and torn apart. Flood waters raced across highways and rail lines. Ten thousand people lost their lives in this monster storm. Millions more were left homeless, penniless, or injured.

Chapter 1

Just fourteen years later in October 2013, another colossal cyclone struck the area: Cyclone Phailin. Wind speeds reached 125 miles an hour. Like the 1999 super-cyclone, the physical damage was severe. More than five hundred thousand homes were damaged, towns were leveled, and electrical grids were destroyed. Amazingly, this time only thirty-nine people lost their lives. Why was there such a significant change in the number of deaths? The people in the area and the governmental leaders were more prepared for Cyclone Phailin. An estimated nine hundred thousand people were evacuated from their homes and sent to shelters in school and government buildings. This evacuation was mandatory, especially for people living in coastal and low-lying areas. Government officials also made sure that the food and medicine that would be needed by the people after the disaster was moved close to the shelters before the cyclone hit. The leaders had a plan and because of that more people were able to survive the storm.

Care Packages at a Time of Need

The day after Hurricane Sandy struck the East Coast of the United States on October 29, 2012, a woman named Celeste Grimes took a morning walk with her children. Her neighborhood in Far Rockaway, Queens, New York, didn't look anything like it had the day before. Seaweed hung from the walls of the local school building. Cars were overturned. Debris was pushed up against houses and sand from the beach covered the street in thick, wavy layers. The Grimes family, like all of the other families in the neighborhood, didn't have running water or electricity in their home. Thus, they had to collect water at a nearby fire hydrant and lug it up eleven flights of stairs to their apartment. Within days, all of the food in their freezer and refrigerator was spoiled. The nearest store that was open for business was almost ten miles away.

The family was particularly grateful for the aid they received from World Vision. They went to their local church and were

After a natural disaster, relief organizations bring food, water, and supplies to people who have lost everything.

Chapter 1

 After Hurricane Sandy, large portions of New York City were without power. Here, only Midtown Manhattan has electricity while many other parts of the city were left in the dark.

surprised to be presented with their own personal hygiene kits (one for each family member) that contained many basic necessities: toothpaste, toothbrush, soap, etc. They also received some home cleaning supplies and a family food kit.

Millions of People Helped Every Year

Anyone who has watched the news in the last few years has witnessed relief efforts such as these firsthand. For example, in November 2013, the most powerful typhoon ever to make landfall struck the islands of the Philippines with nearly two-hundred-mile-per-hour winds. The islands hit were devastated. Cities were completely leveled. Millions upon millions of people were affected directly by the storm—many of them lost everything they owned and had nowhere to live. Soon after the storm subsided, however, relief was on its way. Charitable organizations and governments from around the world immediately sent crews and supplies. In addition, millions of dollars were raised towards the relief effort. In just over one week's time, more than $81 million had been contributed by donors including individuals, organizations, and governments. One-fourth of that, or $20 million, came from the United States.

The US Marines are often some of the first responders on the scene of a natural disaster. Here, they help displaced Philippine nationals at Villamor Air Base in Manila, Philippines, after Typhoon Haiyan in 2013.

CHAPTER 2
Where There's a Need There's a Way

Where there's a need, there's a way—and that is especially true with emergency aid and disaster relief efforts. This emergency aid comes from many different sources. Many governments, especially those who are members of the United Nations, provide disaster-relief aid in the form of money, food, water, supplies, and on-the-ground manpower support. Global charitable organizations are also highly effective in providing aid during times of emergency. Some of these groups have well over a hundred years' worth of experience to pull from and are thus highly organized and efficient in their efforts.

Every disaster is different. Some disasters—like earthquakes, tornadoes, and fires—come on suddenly with little-to-no advanced warning. Other disasters, like typhoons and hurricanes, can be tracked by satellite so people have a few days to prepare for the storm or get out of its path. Just as every natural disaster is different, every place that experiences a disaster is different, too. Some places are better equipped to deal with disasters—the infrastructure is more sound and the government is better organized to handle problems when they occur. In other places, though, the residents are already struggling to meet their basic survival needs. These places often have a poorly organized social and governmental system. For example, according to the Red Cross, one-third of the people who live in the world's urban areas are packed into crowded slums with little-to-no clean water, poor sanitation, inadequate transportation networks, and scanty public and social services. Because of that, these types of areas—and

Advance warning systems can help save lives in any disaster. Bryan Norcross of the Weather Channel discusses a partnership between his station and the National Oceanic and Atmospheric Administration (NOAA). This US government group and other organizations are studying ways to predict severe weather conditions with more accuracy, and with more time to spare.

their residents—are particularly vulnerable when a natural disaster hits.

Therefore, because every situation is so different, organizations that provide disaster relief must carefully assess and evaluate each disaster individually in order to determine the best course of action to follow when providing the necessary emergency aid. The International Federation of Red Cross and Red Crescent Societies provides guidelines for three types of assessments

This is what Seaside Heights, New Jersey, looked like before Hurricane Sandy.

conducted by disaster specialists: rapid assessments, detailed assessments, and continual assessments.

Rapid assessments occur immediately after a disaster occurs, generally within twenty-four to seventy-two hours and sometimes can take about a week to complete. During this evaluation, disaster specialists will look at the condition of the area before and after the disaster. An area might look like it was completely devastated by a hurricane because there are no structures left

This is what Seaside Heights, New Jersey, looked like after Hurricane Sandy.

Chapter 2

standing or the structures are in disrepair. However, maybe there were never any structures in that area to begin with, or only a few poorly-built ones, so the damage is really minimal instead of catastrophic. It's also important to look at how the people's overall livelihood in the area was affected. Are they able to meet their basic needs? What is the current state of wellbeing of the people? This includes their physical and mental health, their nutrition, their access to clean water, sanitation, and housing. Are the people able to protect themselves, or is there a state of lawlessness because of the disaster? Once all of these questions have been answered, the organizers are able to develop an initial plan of action.

Detailed assessments come next. These generally take about a month to complete depending upon the size of the area that was affected and the scope of the damage. During this time, organizers visit many different sites and evaluate the damage and needs of those areas. They also interview a variety of people, including local residents and experts, to get their perspectives on the situation. From all this information, they put together a "detailed" plan as to how they can best help the area on a longer term and broader scale.

Continual assessments are just what the name implies: continual or ongoing. Once the organizations have started their relief efforts, people on the ground constantly evaluate the situation as it progresses or changes. For example, let's say that a disaster relief organization is in the field handing out food in a particular area. After being there for a few days, the organizers find out that there are more people in need of food in a neighboring community. The organizers either split up their staff and send part of the group to the other area to hand out food, or they arrange for more volunteers to help in that area.

Reuniting with Loved Ones

Most of the time, disaster-struck areas that require emergency aid will have the following needs: food, shelter, medical care, safe drinking water, sanitation and waste disposal, essential items like blankets, heaters, and water containers, some form of trauma counseling by mental health professionals, and physical safety from both the elements and from lawlessness. Disaster-relief organizations also help to reunite families. Many times, families will not be together when a disaster strikes. Let's say that on one particular day, the parents in a family are at work and the children are at school. Or, one parent is shopping, the other parent is taking one child to a soccer game, and another child is at a dance class. Everyone is going about their daily activities. Then, suddenly, an earthquake or tornado strikes. Cell phone networks are congested and roads are blocked off. As would be expected, the family members are very anxious to find out if everyone is okay. Disaster relief organizations are key collaborators in helping family members find out information about their loved ones. Many use twenty-first century technology and social networking to do this. For example, the Red Cross offers a service called "Safe and Well." This is a website which allows people to list themselves as "safe and well" if they are in an area that has experienced a natural disaster. Then, family members can go to the Safe and Well website and search for their family member's name to find out whether they're okay. But what if a person doesn't have electricity or access to the Internet after a disaster? Fortunately, electricity (powered by generators) and access to the Internet is often available at evacuation shelters following a disaster.

Following the 2010 earthquake that devastated much of Haiti, many evacuees were brought to the United States by the American Red Cross.

CHAPTER 3
Top Helpers

There are many charitable organizations throughout the world that offer emergency aid and disaster relief. One of the best known is the Red Cross. This organization was founded by a Swiss man named Henry Dunant as a way to help those wounded in war. He had the idea for an international relief organization to bring aid to wounded soldiers after witnessing the Battle of Solferino in Northern Italy in 1859. After fine-tuning his idea for almost four years, Dunant officially founded the International Committee for Relief to the Wounded (later called the International Committee of the Red Cross) in Geneva, Switzerland, on February 9, 1863. Nearly twenty years later, the American Red Cross was founded by a woman named Clara Barton on May 21, 1881, in Washington, DC. The first official disaster relief effort performed by the American Red Cross was just a few months later on September 4 when the organization aided people whose homes were destroyed in forest fires in Michigan.

Today, the American Red Cross works in coordination with the global Red Cross and Red Crescent network (and other partners) to help out in all types of disasters. From July 2012 to June 2013 alone, they helped people in twenty-four countries who needed emergency assistance after earthquakes, floods, tropical storms (like hurricanes and typhoons), droughts, and other disasters. On average, the American Red Cross helps around one hundred million people around the globe every year.

The Salvation Army is another well-known organization that helps people in need. This charity was founded in 1865 by a Christian minister in England named William Booth. His goal at

Clara Barton first worked as a nurse in the Civil War. Then, twenty years later, she started the American Red Cross as a way to help those who had been affected by war, natural disasters, and other crises.

the time was merely to preach the gospel of Jesus Christ to the poor and destitute people of his city who were not typically "socially welcome" in regular church services. Soon, Booth began providing more than spiritual nourishment to his new flock when he began addressing their dire physical needs, too. Over the years, the Salvation Army has continued helping people in need.

The Salvation Army lends a hand to those who have lost everything in natural disasters.

The organization is known today for emergency aid and disaster relief, among other services. When severe floods hit Jakarta and the nearby areas in Indonesia in January 2013, for example, the Salvation Army sent its crews to help. The organization provided the people in the area with food and clean water, boats for transportation, medical supplies, and medical help from doctors

Chapter 3

and nurses. The group also helped when the opposite problem occurred in western India in May 2013. That region hadn't received rain for a long period of time and crops could not grow, resulting in a food shortage. The Salvation Army provided food and water for the people living in those areas just as they had in the areas hit by floods in Indonesia.

Like the Salvation Army, there are many other faith-based organizations that provide aid for victims of natural disasters and other types of emergencies. Most of these charities provide help to people regardless of their religion. As the World Vision website states, "World Vision is a Christian humanitarian organization dedicated to working with children, families, and their communities worldwide. . . . serving all people, regardless of religion, race, ethnicity, or gender." The same is echoed by Islamic Relief USA. A representative from this organization says, "We do not look at race, religion, or any other party or faction. We simply help those in need." Take a look at "On the Internet" in the back of this book for a list of the websites of some of the top faith-based organizations that provide emergency aid all over the world.

Many other nonprofit organizations also provide disaster-relief assistance on a global scale. These include AmeriCares, UNICEF, Doctors Without Borders, Team Rubicon, International Medical Corps, Action Against Hunger, Save the Children, and World Food Programme.

Each of these organizations is prepared to fill specific needs in critical situations. For instance, Doctors Without Borders focuses on providing quality medical care to people in crisis. Action Against Hunger (an organization that aims to eliminate global hunger) centers its efforts on providing food and water to people who have just experienced a major natural disaster or other emergency. Save the Children's mission is to give every child the chance to be healthy, to have an opportunity to learn, and to be able to grow up in a safe environment. When natural disasters strike, this group makes a concerted effort to assess the needs of

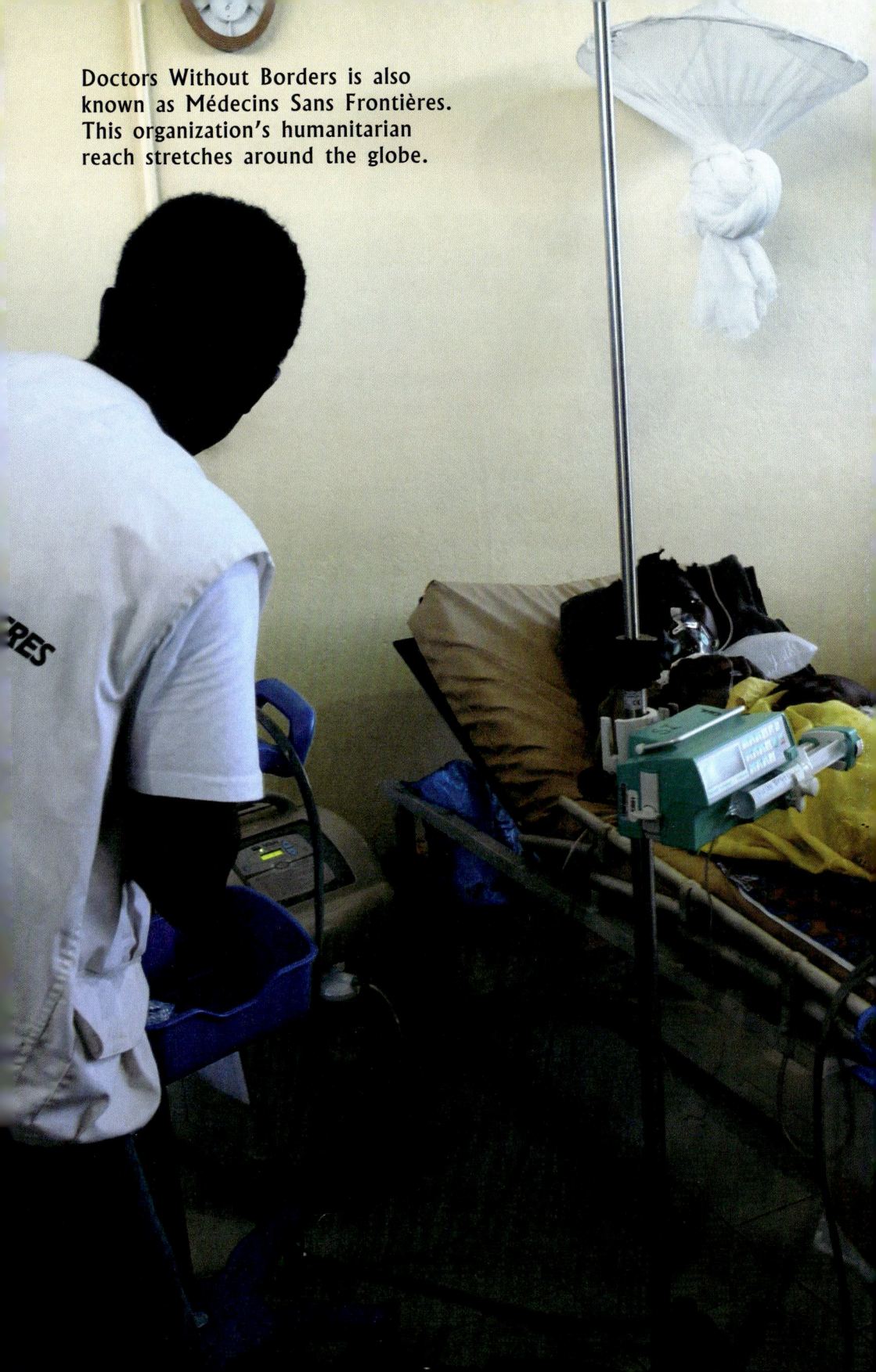

Doctors Without Borders is also known as Médecins Sans Frontières. This organization's humanitarian reach stretches around the globe.

Chapter 3

children in the area and offer aid that is unique to them and their families.

Typhoon Haiyan brought mass devastation to the people of the Philippines in November 2013. Around the world, charitable organizations immediately leaped in to help. Here's a brief description of what some of these groups did:

- The World Food Programme is a United Nations organization that helps fight global hunger. After Typhoon Haiyan, it sent forty metric tons of fortified biscuits to the Philippines.
- Action Against Hunger provided drinking water, buckets, soap, chlorine tablets, and sanitation equipment.
- Save the Children sent items for families and children such as school supplies and household cleaning items. They also provided temporary learning spaces while they repaired schools that had been damaged.
- World Vision provided food, water, and hygiene kits to families at shelters.
- Doctors Without Borders sent two hundred tons of medical supplies and deployed many medical crews.
- Catholic Relief Services provided temporary housing, water, and toilets.
- Red Cross volunteers delivered relief supplies to the area, and helped people find their missing family members. The organization provided hot meals to thousands of people. The Red Cross also delivered tools and building materials to help the community rebuild.
- AmeriCares sent medical supplies for about twenty thousand people, including wound care kits, antibiotics, and pain relievers.

Symbols That Equal Help

Many organizations are recognizable by their unique colors and symbols. The Red Cross, for example, uses a white rectangle with a red cross in the center as its logo. When people see this symbol on buildings, tents, flags, or people's jackets, they know that it means "help is available at this place or from this person."

Another organization that has a specific symbol is the Church of Jesus Christ of Latter-day Saints' (aka Mormon) "Helping Hands" group. The people who help out with this organization, both members of the LDS church and members of the community, wear bright yellow vests which are embellished on the back and chest with a handprint logo. The bright yellow color allows these helpers to stand out in a crowd. Therefore, when survivors of a disaster see groups sporting yellow vests, they know that help has arrived.

The Salvation Army is another organization with a clearly identifiable symbol. This charity uses the color red (like the Red Cross), but its symbol is a shield instead of a cross. Salvation Army volunteers are also known for the hand bells that they ring in front of department stores during the Christmas season, reminding people to donate their extra change to the red-kettle holiday charity drive.

Many other charitable organizations have unique colors and symbols, too. The organization CARE uses a circle made of orange and yellow hands. Save the Children's symbol is a red circle with a line drawing of a child in the center. Since World Vision is a Christian humanitarian aid organization, its logo is an orange corner of a rectangle with a glowing white cross in the center.

CHAPTER 4
Getting Prepared

The Red Cross says that the number of global natural disasters each year has been steadily increasing since the 1970s. While that fact is disheartening, it's encouraging to know that the number of lives lost in major disasters each year has actually *decreased.* How is that possible? Well, experts believe that deaths have decreased because many disaster-prone areas have become better prepared. For one, many communities now have advanced warning systems in place which help people know to evacuate an area when a disaster (like a hurricane or typhoon) is on its way. In addition, organizations, schools, and governments around the world now have better plans to cope with disasters when they strike.

The Red Cross spends a significant amount of time and money helping people prepare for disasters. They want to build "safer, more resilient communities in disaster-prone countries." These communities can adapt to and recover from disasters in a more effective way because they already have emergency shelters and evacuation plans in place in their communities. Their people and leaders are better prepared to deal with disasters. They have strong social networks established and have a more secure economic base.

In order to help communities become more resilient, the Red Cross (and other disaster-relief organizations) conduct trainings with local leaders and community members throughout the world. From July 2012 to June 2013, the Red Cross helped prepare communities in thirty-two countries for future disasters. That doesn't mean that the communities will not experience any loss

Planning ahead can help save lives in a disaster. In the Cook Islands, coastal areas that are susceptible to tsunamis must have specific evacuation routes that lead residents to safer ground. Routes are marked with signs like this one, making it easy for people to know where to go.

Chapter 4

of life or property should a disaster strike their area. But what it does mean is that when calamities come their way, these prepared places will have the infrastructure in place and the trained experts in their own communities to take care of their citizens' needs before outside help can arrive. This greatly increases the chances of survival for injured people and helps a community get back on its feet much more quickly.

One way the Red Cross helps communities get prepared is by planting trees in areas that are prone to floods or landslides. Why trees, you might ask? Well, the roots of trees and other plants help hold soil in place so that when it is soaked with rain it won't wash away. If a slippery slope without any vegetation on it is saturated with a lot of rainfall, the soil—which has now turned into heavy mud—will zip right down the hillside towards the homes below. However, if there are trees and other types of vegetation like grasses and bushes planted on the slope, then the plants will act as a buffer for the rain (absorbing some of it before it reaches the soil), and hold the soil in place to prevent it from shifting.

Disaster relief organizations also help communities improve their drainage systems and river embankments. This prevents the flooding that can occur when a river overflows its banks after heavy precipitation. In addition, these specialists also help people improve community buildings so that the structures are better able to withstand damage during a disaster.

Disaster relief organizations also help communities develop their own disaster plans. To get started, the disaster relief experts will sit down with community leaders and help them think about possible scenarios and the ways their community might be able to handle them. For example, the community leaders first ask themselves some crucial questions:

- What would happen if a particular type of disaster were to strike our area?
- What kind of damage is possible?
- How many structures could be destroyed?

GETTING PREPARED

Sandbags are a crucial disaster preparedness tool. They are used along river banks as a temporary levee. By raising the height of the banks, the sandbags help prevent the river from overflowing and flooding the surrounding areas.

- How many people could be injured?
- How would we respond to the disaster in a quick and efficient way?
- If our communication systems were down, what would we do?
- What kind of safe places do we have for people to seek shelter?
- Do we have evacuation routes clearly labeled and identified so people know how to get out of an area before and during an emergency?
- How would we help people who are injured or suddenly homeless?
- How would we start the cleanup process?

Chapter 4

 Indonesian National Search and Rescue team members simulate a water disaster rescue. Since the country is made up of many islands, water training is important to keep the country prepared.

Once the community leaders answer these types of questions, they are able to come up with a plan to address problem areas. They may establish new emergency shelters for people to come to during and after an emergency. They decide which routes are best for their people to follow during mandatory evacuations. They may offer additional training to medical personnel so these professionals can more efficiently and effectively help people who are injured. The Red Cross helps train members of the community to use basic first-aid techniques. Most often, the very first responders on a scene after a natural disaster are literally the next-door neighbors. If that neighbor knows how to do basic first aid (taking care of neck or spine injuries, performing CPR, or helping a person who is bleeding, in shock, or unconscious), then the chance of an injured person surviving is much greater. Community leaders also consider improving their infrastructure (roads, sanitation systems, etc.) so that if an emergency does occur it won't completely debilitate the community.

Ham Radio to the Rescue

One problem that arises during a disaster is that people may not be able to reach others using the usual lines of communication. Oftentimes, electricity is knocked out. Cell towers are destroyed. People are always able to communicate, however, through ham radio. What is ham radio? No, it's not a communication device made out of pork products. But that's a funny thought. Ham radio is another name for amateur radio. Ham radio does not need electricity to run (there are battery powered ham radios and even hand-powered ones) and they operate on their own radio waves so they're not bound by the limits that other devices (like landline telephones and cell phones) have. Ham radio operators are amateurs. That means that they are people who are interested in radio communication purely as a hobby, not as a career.

"Hams" (as ham radio operators are called) are organized into groups such as the Amateur Radio Emergency Service (ARES). Many disaster relief and emergency aid organizations work with these groups before and after an emergency, and have formal agreements with amateur radio groups. These organizations include Citizen Corps, Federal Emergency Management Agency (FEMA), the American Red Cross, the Salvation Army, and the Association of Public Safety Communications Officials.

Many communities throughout the world are realizing how important it is to have ham radio operators trained and equipped in their area. Following Typhoon Haiyan in the Philippines in 2013, the Philippine Amateur Radio Association (PARA) put in requests for better emergency communication gear. They realized that some of the harder-to-reach areas of the country would also benefit from ham radio equipment and operators to relay and receive critical information.

CHAPTER 5
Lending a Hand

It's Saturday morning and you get a telephone call from someone saying he is part of a charity for disaster relief. "Will you please donate some money to help the people in Oklahoma who just experienced a major tornado?" he asks. "We can take your debit or credit card number right now on the phone."

You really want to help. You have been watching the tornado coverage on the news and you feel really badly for the people in this area. So, what should you do? Is it a good idea to give this person money over the phone? What happens if this person had contacted you by text, social media, or email instead? Would any of those be okay?

The answer in any of those situations is most definitely **NO**! You have no way of knowing for sure if this person who is contacting you is really who he claims he is. He could actually be a person who is using this disaster as an excuse to take money from people for himself or his company. Now, that isn't *for sure* what is happening, but it *could* be and you just can't take the risk. Instead of giving money to this person over the phone, it is best to do your own research and then contact the charity that you would like to donate money to.

So, how do you know if a disaster relief organization is trustworthy? One way is to go to the Better Business Bureau's (BBB) website and find out if the organization has a good solid business reputation. The BBB has a page just for charities at http://www.bbb.org/us/charity/. You will find lots of useful information on this site, including how the charity uses the money it receives. In addition, the BBB's website gives information

It's never a good idea to give money or personal information to someone who calls you on the phone. You don't know who they are or if they will use the money the way that they promise to.

Chapter 5

on complaints about charities, and whether those complaints were resolved. You can also visit Charity Navigator's website (http://www.charitynavigator.org/) to search out a particular disaster relief organization's name and see how it is ranked. If a charity has a low ranking, it's best to steer clear. Likewise, you can also visit Charity Watch (http://www.charitywatch.org/) and GuideStar (http://www.guidestar.org/). These organizations research charities as well, and provide their own rankings to the public on their websites.

After you have made sure that a disaster relief organization is on the up and up, what should you do next? Well, experts say that the *best* type of donation is always a monetary donation. That's because the disaster relief specialists can often buy the products and supplies needed at a better rate (since they are buying in bulk) and they also have a better idea of exactly what is needed. In addition, they often purchase supplies from areas that are nearby the disaster zone. That way, shipping costs are reduced and the local economy is helped too.

One donation that is *always* frowned upon in disaster relief situations is old clothing and other miscellaneous items. Imagine being a person who is in need of disaster relief and receiving a box full of Santa Claus costumes and half-used tubes of toothpaste. This might sound ridiculous, but it's actually something that happened! Disaster relief specialists call these donations the "second disaster." Not only does it not do any good to send boxes and boxes full of things that people cannot use—it can actually make a bad situation worse. Boxes of supplies that can't be used just end up clogging the entire system and preventing the necessary supplies from reaching the people who need them. Instead of sending used clothing, it's a better idea to have a yard sale and then send the money earned to a disaster relief organization to use in the emergency effort.

In addition to getting involved with disaster relief *after* a disaster, people can also help out *before* a disaster. For one, they can get trained in first aid to learn how to take care of people who

> Yard sales and lemonade stands are great ways to earn money to donate to disaster relief organizations.

are injured. They can also learn how to perform CPR so they can help if a person isn't breathing. These skills are *extremely* helpful in an emergency situation, especially for a person who may want to travel to the disaster area and offer volunteer assistance.

Another way that ordinary people can help is by getting their amateur radio license. That way, if communications are no longer working in an area, these "hams" can help relay messages back and forth to help government officials and disaster relief specialists in the relief effort. To find out where classes are offered in your area, visit the National Association for Amateur Radio's website at http://www.arrl.org/.

People can also help out by making personal hygiene kits and donating these to relief organizations. A personal hygiene kit is generally a large gallon-size zipper storage bag that is packed with such things as soap, toothbrushes, toothpaste, washcloths, shampoo and body wash, lotion, deodorant, etc. When a disaster strikes, these kits (which are already assembled and stored by disaster relief organizations) are then sent out immediately to the people in need. Many groups around the nation enjoy assembling these kits as service projects: church groups make them, youth groups and

Assembling disaster relief kits is one way that youth organizations can help out before a disaster even occurs.

school groups make them, and scouting groups make them. Sometimes the groups themselves purchase all of the items for the personal hygiene kits while other times they ask businesses and individuals to donate money or items for the kits. Before you begin, decide which organization you will donate your kits to. Be sure to contact them to make sure they accept these donations, and to find out exactly what should be in each hygiene kit.

So, how will you help out in a disaster? Will you sell lemonade and donate the proceeds to a charity? Will you volunteer to pack food items into boxes at a disaster relief warehouse? Will you take courses to get your ham radio operator license? Will you plan an event where your friends and neighbors get together to assemble personal hygiene kits?

Regardless of which action you take to help, your service will be greatly appreciated by someone somewhere. It will also help you feel pretty great, too. As the philosopher Albert Schweitzer once said, "I don't know what your destiny will be, but one thing I know: The ones among you who will be really happy are those who have sought and found how to serve."

Send in the Troops — The US Military Helps Out with Disaster Relief

Members of the United States military are often some of the first responders on the scene of global natural disasters. That's because US military men and women are stationed throughout the world. Many of our aircraft carriers are also conveniently located in various global ports and can be deployed immediately if and when they're needed. Generally, within hours or days of a calamity, the Marines can be on the ground delivering relief supplies and helping with search and rescue operations. The US Navy's aircraft carriers are usually a close second to arrive.

These carriers are a very helpful resource for areas struck by disaster. They can hold thousands of people, including medical staff and others with specialized training. In addition to a highly-skilled crew, carriers and the ships like destroyers and cruisers that accompany them also have a wide variety of transportation equipment that can be used in relief efforts. These vessels also bring much-needed food, water, and medical supplies to the area. An awesome bonus is that carriers have onboard desalination plants that can transform seawater into drinking water.

In November 2013 following Typhoon Haiyan, the Navy aircraft carrier USS *George Washington* moored off the east of Samar Island in the Philippines. The carrier had approximately sixty aircraft onboard, and twenty-one of them were helicopters. These choppers were especially useful for transporting supplies to areas that were inaccessible by land. The five-thousand-member crew helped in search and rescue operations and assisted local authorities as needed. The USS *George Washington* was also able to supply the area with four hundred thousand gallons of freshwater every day.

The US military provides supplies to places that have suffered disasters.

WHAT YOU CAN DO TO HELP

There are many ways that kids and teens can get involved in emergency aid and disaster relief. Here are some of our top suggestions:

- Get Certified in First Aid and CPR: The Red Cross offers classes in many locations throughout the country. To find out more, visit their website at http://www.redcross.org/take-a-class/.

- Get Licensed in Amateur Radio: The National Association for Amateur Radio offers their licensing class throughout the year. Find the next scheduled class in your area by visiting: http://www.arrl.org/find-an-amateur-radio-license-class. Most of these classes are free of charge, although you will need to buy one of the handbooks.

- Raise Funds: Money is the best commodity to donate after a disaster. Kids and teens can raise money in many different ways, with an adult's permission and help, of course. Some ideas include having a bake sale, car wash, lemonade stand, yard sale, or charity drive. Make signs that say what the money will be used for ("Helping Typhoon Survivors in the Philippines") and make sure *all* of the money is used for that purpose!

- Make Personal Hygiene Kits: These kits are widely needed after a disaster, and *before* a disaster is the best time to make them so they're ready to be sent immediately to the people in need. Many organizations collect them. To find the most current listing of organizations, conduct a Google search with these words: "Personal Hygiene Kits."

- Donate Food to Your Local Food Pantry: A well-stocked food pantry is essential at all times. If an area that is struck by a disaster already has a large food supply, it will be able to cope much better with a disaster (should one strike).

TIMELINE

816	A typhoon that hits northern China is the earliest recorded typhoon to make landfall in the country.
1348	An earthquake strikes northeastern Italy, destroying towns, and killing hundreds.
1859	The Battle of Solferino inspires Henry Dunant to form the Red Cross.
1863	The Red Cross (then known as the International Committee for Relief to the Wounded) is officially founded by Henry Dunant in Geneva, Switzerland.
1865	The Salvation Army is founded by William Booth in England.
1881	The American Red Cross is founded by Clara Barton in Washington, DC. The organization helps people in Michigan whose homes were destroyed by forest fires.
1921–1923	American Relief Administration sends food to Russia where drought and civil war have caused widespread famine.
1941	President Franklin D. Roosevelt signs the Lend-Lease Act. This program sends aid to countries in the form of weapons, clothing, vehicles, and food. Approximately $50 billion in supplies is shipped out.
1946	The United Nations founds UNICEF to help European children affected by World War II.
1950	World Vision is founded to bring awareness to the children living in poverty around the world.
1979	The Federal Emergency Management Agency (FEMA) is created, a US government organization with the mission "to lead America to prepare for, prevent, respond to, and recover from disasters."
1983–1985	Drought in Ethiopia claims the lives of more than four hundred thousand people. "Live Aid" concert in Philadelphia and London help raise awareness and money for fighting hunger in Africa. More than $140 million is raised.
1992	US troops and supplies are sent to Somalia to assist with the humanitarian relief of the country's famine-stricken people.
1994–1998	One million people die in North Korea after extreme flooding and famine. The US government provides the country with more than $900 million worth of food and supplies.
1999	A super-cyclone strikes India killing ten thousand and leaving thousands more homeless, penniless, and injured.
2010	An earthquake in Haiti kills hundreds of thousands of people, and leaves over one million others homeless. Billions of dollars are donated as many organizations arrive to assist the surviving residents, including the Red Cross and Doctors Without Borders.
2012	EF2 tornado snakes through Branson, Missouri, with swirling winds at 120-130 miles per hour. Hurricane Sandy hits the East Coast of the United States.
2013	The USS George Washington, two cruisers, and a destroyer aid the Philippines in disaster relief after Typhoon Haiyan.
2014	US federal government grants $102.7 million to eleven eastern states for disaster preparedness projects.

FURTHER READING

Books
Benge, Janet and Geoff. *Clara Barton: Courage Under Fire.* Lynnwood, WA: Emerald Books, 2012.
Bradley, Arthur T. *Handbook to Practical Disaster Preparedness for the Family.* New York: Skyhorse Publishing, 2012.
Courtley, Cade. *SEAL Survival Guide: A Navy Seal's Secrets to Surviving Any Disaster.* New York: Gallery Books, 2012.
Irwin, Julia F. *Making the World Safe: The American Red Cross and a Nation's Humanitarian Awakening.* New York: Oxford University Press, 2013.
Kolberg, Judith. *Organize for Disaster: Prepare Your Family and Your Home for Any Natural Disaster.* Decatur, GA: Squall Press, 2005.
Saubers, Nadine. *The Everything First Aid Book.* Avon, MA: Adams Media, 2008.
Silver, H. Ward. *Ham Radio for Dummies.* Hoboken, NJ: John Wiley & Sons, 2013.

On the Internet
American Red Cross: Safe and Well
https://safeandwell.communityos.org/cms/index.php
Bullitt Amateur Radio Society
http://www.ky4ky.com/yhn.htm
Ready.gov: Be A Hero
http://www.ready.gov/kids
Ready.gov: Free Publications
http://www.ready.gov/publications

Disaster-Relief Organizations
Action Against Hunger
http://www.actionagainsthunger.org/
American Red Cross
http://www.redcross.org/
AmeriCares
http://www.americares.org/
Doctors Without Borders
http://www.doctorswithoutborders.org/
International Medical Corps
http://internationalmedicalcorps.org/
National Voluntary Organizations Active in Disaster
http://www.nvoad.org/
Salvation Army
http://salvationarmyusa.org/
Save the Children
http://savethechildren.org/
Team Rubicon
http://teamrubiconusa.org/
UNICEF
http://www.unicefusa.org/
World Food Programme
http://www.wfp.org/

Faith-Based Organizations
American Jewish Joint Distribution Committee
http://www.jdc.org/
Buddhist Global Relief
http://www.buddhistglobalrelief.org/
Catholic Relief Services
http://crs.org/
Church of Jesus Christ of Latter-day Saints (LDS) Philanthropies
http://www.ldsphilanthropies.org/
Islamic Relief USA
http://www.irusa.org/tag/disaster-relief/
Lutheran World Relief
http://lwr.org/
World Vision
http://www.worldvision.org/

Works Consulted
Alexander, Jessica. "Please Don't Send Your Old Shoes to the Philippines." *Slate*, November 11, 2013. http://www.slate.com/articles/news_and_politics/foreigners/2013/11/how_to_help_typhoon_haiyan_survivors_in_the_philippines_the_only_donation.html
American Red Cross. "CPR/AED Awareness Week: Get Trained." June 3, 2013. http://www.redcross.org/news/article/CPRAED-Awareness-Week-Get-Trained
American Red Cross. "Disaster Preparedness." http://www.redcross.org/what-we-do/international-services/disaster-preparedness
American Red Cross. *Global Impact Report, Fiscal Year 2012.* http://www.redcross.org/images/MEDIA_CustomProductCatalog/m15640241_globalimpactreport2012.pdf
American Red Cross. "Recovering after a Disaster or Emergency." http://www.redcross.org/find-help/disaster-recovery
American Red Cross. "Responding to Disasters Overseas." http://www.redcross.org/what-we-do/international-services/responding-disasters-overseas
BBC News Asia. "Typhoon Haiyan: US Carrier Boosts Philippines Relief Effort." November 14, 2013. http://www.bbc.co.uk/news/world-asia-24936387

FURTHER READING

BBC News India. "Cyclone Phailin: India Intensifies Relief Efforts." October 16, 2013. http://www.bbc.co.uk/news/world-asia-india-24546015

Chandwani, Karuna. "Cyclone Phailin: World Bank Team Visit Odisha to Assess Damage and Assist with $313 Million." *International Business Times, India,* November 28, 2013. http://www.ibtimes.co.in/articles/525885/20131128/odisha-cyclone-phailin-ganjam-world-bank-funds.htm

Charity Navigator. "Super Typhoon Haiyan Disaster Relief." November 8, 2013. http://www.charitynavigator.org/index.cfm?bay=content.view&cpid=1659#.UplOOcRaUpk

Charity Navigator. "What To Do When A Charity Calls." http://www.charitynavigator.org/index.cfm/bay/content.view/catid/68/cpid/224.htm#.UplO9MRaUpk

Federal Trade Commission (FTC). "Before Giving to a Charity." *Consumer Information.* http://www.consumer.ftc.gov/articles/0074-giving-charity

Gast, Phil. "Resort City of Branson Takes a Direct Hit from Tornado." CNN, February 29, 2012. http://www.cnn.com/2012/02/29/us/missouri-branson-storm/

Hickey, Walter. "Infographic: Aircraft Carriers Do a Whole Lot More Than You Ever Thought." *Business Insider,* June 15, 2012. http://www.businessinsider.com/infographic-air-craft-carriers-do-a-whole-lot-more-than-shoot-2012-6

Huffington Post. "How To Help Typhoon Haiyan Survivors." November 9, 2013. http://www.huffingtonpost.com/2013/11/09/philippines-haiyan-how-to-help-_n_4247106.html

Hunter, Melissa. "UGA Red Cross Club Teaches 90 Students Hands-Only CPR." American Red Cross, East Georgia Chapter, April 1, 2013. http://redcrossresults.wordpress.com/2013/04/01/uga-red-cross-club-teaches-90-students-hands-only-cpr/

International Federation of Red Cross and Red Crescent Societies. *Guidelines for Assessment in Emergencies.* March 2008. https://www.ifrc.org/Global/Publications/disasters/guidelines/guidelines-emergency.pdf

Kapur, Mallika and David Simpson. "Cyclone Phailin: India Relieved at Low Death Toll." CNN, October 14, 2013. http://www.cnn.com/2013/10/14/world/asia/india-cyclone-phailin/

Monroe News. "A Friend for Life: Monroe Teen's Actions Help Save Man from Heart Attack." January 6, 2012. http://www.monroenews.com/news/2012/jan/06/a-friend-for-life/

The National Association for Amateur Radio. "Find an Amateur Radio License Class." http://www.arrl.org/find-an-amateur-radio-license-class

The National Association for Amateur Radio. "Hams Up Their Game in Philippines Typhoon Response." November 20, 2013. http://www.arrl.org/news/hams-up-their-game-in-philippines-typhoon-response

Pickert, Kate. "A Brief History of the Salvation Army." *Time,* December 2, 2008. http://content.time.com/time/nation/article/0,8599,1863162,00.html

Reinhardt, Laura. "Grateful Survivor Tells Donors: 'Thank You for Being Epic.'" World Vision US Programs. http://www.worldvisionusprograms.org/disaster-response-grateful-survivor-superstorm-sandy.php

The Salvation Army International. "Current Emergency Responses." http://www.salvationarmy.org/ihq/iesresponses#INT0113

The Salvation Army International. "History." http://www.salvationarmy.org/ihq/history

The Salvation Army International. "Our Work." http://www.salvationarmy.org/ihq/ourwork

Silva, Daniella. "Typhoon Haiyan: A Crisis by the Numbers." NBC News, November 17, 2013. http://worldnews.nbcnews.com/_news/2013/11/17/21496134-typhoon-haiyan-a-crisis-by-the-numbers?lite

Tressler, Colleen. "How to Help Victims of Typhoon Haiyan in the Philippines." *Consumer Information,* Federal Trade Commission (FTC), November 12, 2013. http://www.consumer.ftc.gov/blog/how-help-victims-typhoon-haiyan-philippines

When Disaster Strikes, Send the Enterprise. "Home." http://www.sendtheenterprise.org/

World Vision. "Who We Are." http://www.worldvision.org/about-us/who-we-are

GLOSSARY

aircraft carrier—A large flat topped ship that is used by the military to transport sailors and aircraft.

coordination (koh-awr-din-EY-shuhn)—Working together harmoniously.

cyclone (SAHY-klohn)—A storm made up of low-pressure winds that spin in a circle with a center eye. Cyclones occur in the South Pacific and Indian Ocean, and are called hurricanes in the Atlantic and Northeastern Pacific oceans, and typhoons in the Northwestern Pacific Ocean.

debris (duh-BREE)—Fragments of manmade or natural materials that have been broken up and scattered.

drought (drowt)—A long period of little or no rainfall.

earthquake (URTH-kweyk)—Sudden violent shaking of the ground caused by the movements of rocks or magma beneath the surface of the earth.

evacuation (ih-vak-yoo-EY-shuhn)—The act of leaving a place when a natural disaster (like a hurricane) is approaching.

hurricane (HER-ih-kayn)—A cyclone that occurs in the Atlantic or Northeastern Pacific oceans.

hygiene (HAHY-jeen)—Practices such as body washing, hand washing, teeth cleaning, and clothes washing that help a person maintain health and cleanliness.

lawlessness—A state of disorder where people do not follow the rules or laws.

tornado (tawr-NEY-doh)—Violently rotating winds that form a funnel-shaped cloud.

typhoon (tahy-FOON)—A cyclone that occurs in the Northwestern Pacific Ocean.

volcanic eruption (vol-KAN-ik ih-RUHP-shuhn)—The occurrence of molten lava or other volcanic material pushing itself out of a break in the earth's surface called a volcano.

PHOTO CREDITS: All design elements from Photos.com/Sharon Beck; Cover, p. 1—ABACA/Newscom; pp. 4, 11—Americanspirit/Dreamstime ; p. 7—Todd Feeback/MCT/Newscom; p. 8—Wellphotos/Dreamstime; p. 9—US National Oceanic and Atmospheric Administration; p. 12—David Shankbone; p. 13—Lance Cpl. Caleb Hoover/US Department of Defense; p. 15—Mark Wilson/Getty Images; pp. 16-17—Edward Crimmins/Getty; pp. 18-19—Electrochris/Dreamstime; p. 21—Joe Burbank/MCT/Newscom; p. 23—Photos.com/Thinkstock; pp. 24-25—Fernando Salazar/MCT/Newscom; p. 27—Issouf Sanogo/AFP/Getty Images/Newscom; p. 29—Jtasphoto/Dreamstime; p. 31—Lucidwaters Dreamstime; p. 33—Patsy Lynch/FEMA; p. 34—Mohammed Asad/ZUMA Press/Newscom; p. 35—macbrianmun/Thinkstock; p. 37—moodboard/Thinkstock; p. 39—David Sacks/Thinkstock; p. 40—Christopher Mardorf/FEMA; p. 41—Seaman Chris Cavagnaro/US Department of Defense

INDEX

Action Against Hunger   26, 28
aircraft carriers   41
amateur radio   35, 39, 40
American Red Cross   5, 8–9, 21, 22, 23, 35
AmeriCares   26, 28
assessments   16–17, 20
Barton, Clara   22–23
Battle of Solferino   22
Better Business Bureau (BBB)   36, 38
Booth, William   22, 24
Branson, Missouri   6, 7
CARE   29
Catholic Relief Services   28
Charity Navigator   38
Charity Watch   38
chemical spills   5
Church of Jesus Christ of Latter-day Saints   29
continual assessments   17, 20
CPR   6, 8–9, 34, 39
cyclones   9, 10
detailed assessments   17, 20
Doctors Without Borders   26, 27, 28
donations   36, 37, 38, 39–40
drainage   32
droughts   5, 22, 26
Dunant, Henry   22
earthquakes   5, 14, 21, 22
electricity   10, 21, 35
evacuation   10, 21, 30, 31, 33, 34
faith-based organizations   10, 12, 22, 24–26, 28, 29
fires   5, 14, 22

first aid   34, 38–39
floods   5, 22, 25, 32
food   6, 10, 11, 14, 21, 25, 26, 28, 41
George Washington (USS)   41
Grimes, Celeste   10
GuideStar   38
Haiti   21
Haiyan, Typhoon   13, 28, 35, 41
Hammer, Jim   8
ham radio (*see* amateur radio)
Heiser, Reid   6, 8–9
hurricanes   5, 10, 12, 14, 17, 18–19, 22
hygiene items   6, 12, 28, 39–40
India   9–10, 26
Indonesia   25–26, 34
International Federation of Red Cross and Red Crescent Societies   16, 22
International Medical Corps   26
Islamic Relief USA   26
locating family members   21, 28
Marines (US)   13, 41
medicine   10, 21, 25–26, 27, 28, 41
military   13, 41
Mormon Helping Hands   29
National Association of Amateur Radio   39
National Oceanic and Atmospheric Administration (NOAA)   15
Navy (US)   41
New York City   10, 12
Norcross, Bryan   15

Odisha super-cyclone (Cyclone O5B)   9, 10
Phailin, Cyclone   10
Philippines   13, 28, 35, 41
prediction   14, 15
preparedness   10, 14, 16, 30–34
rapid assessments   17
Red Cross   5, 8–9, 14, 16, 21, 22, 23, 28, 29, 30, 32, 34, 35
river embankments   32
Safe and Well   21
Salvation Army   22, 24–26, 29, 35
sandbags   33
Sandy, Hurricane   10, 12, 16–19
Save the Children   26, 28, 29
Schweitzer, Albert   40
Seaside Heights, New Jersey   16–19
shelter   6, 9, 10, 13, 14, 21, 28, 33, 34
social networking   21
symbols   29
Team Rubicon   26
tornadoes   5, 6, 7, 14, 21, 36
trees   32
tsunamis   5, 31
typhoons   5, 13, 14, 22, 28, 30, 35, 41
UNICEF   26
United Nations   14, 28
volcanic eruptions   5
water   10, 11, 14, 21, 25, 26, 28, 41
Weather Channel   15
World Food Programme   26, 28
World Vision   10, 12, 26, 28, 29

About the Author

Amie Jane Leavitt is an accomplished author, researcher, and photographer. She has written more than sixty books and has contributed to online and print media. Amie has a particular interest in emergency aid and disaster relief. She resided in Hawaii in 1992 when Hurricane Iniki pounded the island chain's shores, and because of that had the opportunity to volunteer in a disaster preparedness capacity. For a listing of Amie's current projects and published works, check out her website at www.amiejaneleavitt.com.